God in all I see

a collection of poems

Sarah Lindholm

God in all I see

Published by The Conrad Press in the United Kingdom 2023

Tel: +44(0)1227 472 874
www.theconradpress.com
info@theconradpress.com

ISBN 978-1-915494-48-1

Typesetting and Cover Design by: Charlotte Mouncey, www.bookstyle.co.uk
The Conrad Press logo was designed by Maria Priestley.

Printed and bound in Great Britain by Clays Ltd, Elcograf S.p.A.

Contents

As the seasons change   6

Spring

Life!   8
Growth   9
Water   10
Dandelions   11
Easter Sunday   12
Flight   13
Dawn musings   14
Giver of life   15
A snapshot of time   16

Summer

Creation	18
Wings	19
Sunbeams	20
A place of safety	21
Water lilies	22
Transformation	23
Stones	24
Time	25

Autumn

Autumn	28
Scottish highlands	29
Light	30
Rainclouds	31
Battles at dusk	33
Lighthouse	34
Hope stirring	35
Halloween	36

Winter

Advent	38
Mary	39
Joseph	40
Elizabeth	41
The child	42
Snow	43
Winter wonderland	44
Snowscape	45
The donkey's journey	46
The Light	47
Angels of hope	48
The shepherds	49
Lucia	50
Christmas trees	51
Christmas markets	52
Christmas poem	53
The star	55
Men of wisdom	56
Egypt	57
The innocents	58
Celebration	59
The cornerstone	60
Love at Christmas	61
The visitor	62
Christmas day	63

As the seasons change

Snow into snowdrops,
Daffodils to daylight,
Long sunny days
On the beach at low tide.
Autumn's warm colours,
Red, orange, yellow,
Hearth fires and harvest,
With much more besides.
Conkers and Christmas,
With folks buying presents,
Back into springtime,
Year after year.
Beautiful flowers
That win competitions,
Time spent with loved ones,
Those we hold dear.
May we remember
The good things we're given,
The beauty of creation,
As we watch the seasons change.
May we give honour
To the Person who gave them,
Who, unlike the seasons,
Stays always the same.

Amen.

Spring

Life!

Springtime has come.
Flowers grow and bloom,
The Spirit pours itself out on all flesh.
He comes with freedom,
Light
And LIFE!
He dances with us
And romances our hearts,
Cracked and torn,
Healing while His love
Pours out on us.
We are loved, seen and smiled upon.
Forever.

Amen.

Growth

A seed,
Buried beneath the ground,
Slumbering through winter,
Waiting for the moment
When…
The sun shines down
And rain droplets
Soak steadily into the soil.
The seed wakes up,
Searches for that sun,
Heads towards the surface…
And breaks it, green shoots appearing,
The first sign
Of Spring.

Amen

Water

A drop in the ocean,
A glass from the tap.
Rain, sleet, hail,
A river running by.
A babbling brook,
A calm, still lake.
Snow, causing a landscape of white,
Ice, slipping and sliding,
Skating and gliding,
A dip in the sea,
Cold and unforgiving,
A swim in the pool,
Indoors or outdoors.
Thank You, my Father,
For water, in all its forms.

Amen.

Dandelions

A dandelion clock, its yellow glory replaced by something not even a pale ghost of its former brilliance, a white globe, representing the fleetingness of time, blown by the wind, scattered to the four corners of the earth.

Two planes, their air clouds streaking out behind them, almost looking as if they're racing, trying to outdo each other as they fly across the heavens. The sky in the east is a pale pink, hinting at a cloudless day ahead. Peace reigns in my heart, and the sky is blue and free. I rejoice in my Saviour and sing to my Light as the sun breaks over the horizon, promising a glorious day.

Easter Sunday

Alive!
The day dawns bright and sunny,
The stone is rolled away
And a new life can begin.
He is risen
And I with Him,
My life
Inextricably entwined
With His,
Allowing me to live for Him
Always.

Amen.

Flight

Standing at the edge,
Staring at the rocks below.
I jump, falling towards the mist,
Not knowing what's going to happen.
I wait, praying that my wings will open,
As the rocks loom
Closer and closer.
Then…
I see it.
The key to my heart,
My wings,
Reaching out to catch me.
I love You,
My saviour.

Amen

Dawn musings

Dawn. 6.40am…ish

A silvery mist surrounds everything, giving an eerie sense of stillness, tendrils moving like fingers swirling in and around each other.

I grab my bright red suitcase, somehow incongruous against the mist, and set off. On the way, I see a clump of startlingly yellow daffodils, their trumpets silent… as usual. I try to imagine what tune they would play if their trumpets were real.

The road is relatively clear of cars, making the estate feel ghost-like, like one of those American towns long abandoned.

Spring is much in evidence along the sides of the road, the catkins (or lambs' tails) plentiful.

I am excited for the day, and thank God for being alive, rejoicing in His goodness and feeling ready for anything.

Giver of life

Giver of life
Yet dangerous in quantity,
Roaring down to distant shores.
A drop,
A trickle,
The stream overflowing,
A raging torrent,
Crashing down the mountainside
Until it reaches the calm, placid lake.
So different,
Yet all the same
Life giving,
Thirst quenching
Water.

Amen.

A snapshot of time

A tree, partially flowering, shows its white buds, delicately formed, petals scattered underfoot as the sun shines down upon the square. The stillness is broken by cars, one of them blasting out dance music as it drives by, then silence, just the noise of traffic, as it drives off.

I watch some kids kicking a ball and wonder at the fleetingness of time, as I try to capture this moment in words. The peace in my heart is different to the world's peace, and yet I feel at peace, here in the heart of the city, with its noise and business. I embrace this moment, this life in all its gloriousness and praise God for all the things He has done, is doing and is going to do, one glorious moment at a time.

Summer

Creation

Inky, impenetrable blackness, not a sound to be heard, just…
nothingness, stretching out for miles.

But then… a presence, as if someone changed the void,
beginning to pour Himself out, speaking words of life, the
imperceptible whisper: 'Let there be light.'

A spark, something catching in the depths of that void, then
suddenly an explosion of life, colour and beauty, atoms collid-
ing, elements being formed in the fire of the biggest bang
ever, the beginning of life, caused by four words, changing
everything.

Wings

The dawn was crystal clear, and she gazed out over the cliff, watching the sun rise, her shawl wrapped around her. She could feel His presence behind her, solid as a rock, and leaned back into His arms. He smiled and stroked her cheek gently with one finger, sending a shiver of pleasure down her back.

She turned to face Him, looking up into His scarred yet handsome face, then kissed Him, a kiss that broke down barriers, that spoke volumes in the silence. He took her hand, smiling at her, and together they leapt, their wings unfurling as they dropped, then soaring together, entwining themselves like hawks on the wing, further and further into the atmosphere, then heading into the sunrise to start a new day.

Sunbeams

The sunlight filters through the trees,
Bathing all in dappled light.
You spin in the clearing,
Letting the sunbeams fall
Upon your face,
Delighting in His love,
Drawing close to Him
And feeling one with the nature He created.

Amen

A place of safety

A secluded beach,
A breath-taking view,
A sense of peace in the midst of chaos.
A sheltered harbour,
A mountain lake,
A forest glade,
Full of flowers,
The sunlight filtering through the canopy.
Your arms, resting there,
Knowing who you are,
Who we are,
And giving thanks,
Whatever the circumstance.

Water lilies

Water lilies floating on a lake, their edges pink, as they glide gracefully towards the bank.

A weeping willow stands there, its long green leaves reaching down to touch the water's edge.

The grass around is verdant, dotted with wild flowers. In the distance there is a Greek temple, its columns reaching up to try and touch the sky.

I lie on a rowing boat in the middle, staring at the cloudless blue sky. The song of birds floats peacefully through the atmosphere.

The peace and tranquillity of this place invade my heart, and I feel beautifully at rest.

Transformation

A seed,
Planted in the ground,
So small yet containing
So much inside it.
You water it,
Feed it,
Give it sunlight and protection,
Watch it grow and flourish
As it blooms, unhindered,
Till you have the biggest
Sunflower
In the garden.

Amen

Stones

Smooth as glass
To the touch,
Clasped
In my hand,
Washed clean
By a river,
This stone shimmers
In the grey light of day.
Not quite spherical, it holds
Its own heat.
If it could talk,
I wonder what stories it would tell?

I remember another tale
With stones in,
Also washed by water,
When a giant was toppled
By a shepherd boy,
And remember that
With God, all things are possible.

Time

Time flies on wings
Of golden dreams,
Sailing over happy
Memories,
Joyous seasons of celebration,
Coming to rest on
Oceans of forgotten promises,
Treasures long

Lost

In regret.

Time does not share
The joys,
The sorrows,
The
Heartaches,
But simply
Observes,
Watching impassively,

As we wind our slow
And faithful way
To the place where our
Father
Will greet us with
Open arms
And say,
"Welcome Home,
My child,
My beloved,
My bride."

Autumn

Autumn

Crisp leaves crunching underfoot,
A kaleidoscope of reds, yellows and oranges
With some brown thrown in for good measure.
Harvest displays,
Giant pumpkins
And farmer's produce,
Corn cobs and green beans
The size of our outstretched hand.
Roaring bonfires,
With parkin and marshmallows,
Playing with sparklers till they run out.
Days getting darker,
With dusk at 4pm,
Rushing to get back home
For tea and crumpets
In front of the roaring fire,
Playing with conkers in the playground
And looking forward
To bright blue skies
The next day.

Amen.

Scottish highlands

The mist brushes the hilltops.
I look across acres of pine.
The clouds
Skid
Across the sky,
Showing blueness now and then.
I pass bushes thick with
Red berries,
Seeing houses tucked away behind the trees,
Then drive past fields,
Sheep grazing in them.
Looking back on this
Reminds me of innocence,
A time of joy
And adventure.

Amen.

Light

A candle, flickering
In the dark.
Its tiny
Flame
Sheds a world of light, combating
The shadows
That creep, that encircle it, encroaching closer and closer
As the
Flame
Dies.

Another light, coming to rest,
Brings a fresh perspective,
As the dawn rises
Upon a new day.

Rainclouds

Thunderclouds loom ominously
Overhead
A few
Telltale
Drops
Hitting
The pavement.
Umbrellas go up,
People scurry
Like mice to shelter
From the deluge.

Only one man
Stands
In the middle of the
High Street,
Arms opened wide,
Head
Up,
Waiting for the clouds
To burst,

To drench him with
Living water
And bring him out of this
Dry
And
Barren
Land
Into
Green pastures
Once again.

Battles at dusk

As the sun sinks below the treelined horizon, I try to get a snapshot of that

Elusive moment when the sun

And horizon meet, doing battle with each other,

The horizon winning every time,

To be repeated, though a little different, every time they meet,

Dawn

And dusk.

Lighthouse

From darkness to light,
You have guided us;
Led us by Your hand,
Even when we cannot see our way.

A beacon,
Shining through the night,
Giving hope in the darkness,
Blazing high till the break of day.

Hope stirring

A light,
Shining in the dark,
Warm and comforting,
Banishing the shadows
To the farthest corners
Of the room
And welcoming life,
Love
And peace.
A star among the blackness,
Pointing the way
To Him.

Amen.

Halloween

Ghouls and ghosts
Come out to play,
Calling all spirits,
Just for one day.
Come to the place where the battle was won,
Where Jesus, our saviour, cried,
'It is done!'
So spirits above and below come to play,
But only on this one fateful day,
For God gave His life that we might be free
Of those spirits that torment both you and me.
Ghouls and ghosts
Come out to play,
Calling all spirits,
Just for one day.

Amen

Winter

Advent

A time for preparation,
Getting ready for the Day,
The pastry's done,
The gingerbread too,
Having friends and family here,
All to celebrate His birth,
A time to prepare our hearts and minds,
Let love flow once again,
As it did that Christmas day.

Amen.

Mary

My Son,
Carried in my womb,
A plan created by Father...
And He asks me?
I am but a teenager,
A fourteen-year-old girl,
And the Creator,
My Creator,
Asks me to be
Mother to His Son?
I am in awe,
Amazed and humbled,
So I say
Yes.

Amen.

Joseph

I thought her unfaithful,
Yet she denied it.
I thought with much care
And decided on a course
Of action.
I made up my mind,
Went to sleep and…
Decided to keep her
As my wife.
The child growing inside her
Is more precious
Than jewels or even water
And I will carry out
My God given duty
And privilege
To Him who saves my soul.

Amen.

Elizabeth

The child in me
Jumped
For joy
When He came.
I knew He was special
And Mary was blessed
With His baby
But my bundle of joy
Confirmed it.
I would feel that joy again,
Know in my heart
That He loved me
And gave me His life.

Amen.

The child

To make Yourself small,
A baby,
Craving His mother's milk.
A light,
Clothed in human flesh
And sent for
The outcast;
The leper,
The abused and afflicted.
People on the fringes,
The lost and the broken,
The 'weird' and the wonderful
And all those in between.
Thank You and

Amen.

Snow

Flurries,
Drifts,
Snowballs and men,
Sledging down the hill
In a homemade toboggan.
Scarves,
Coats and hats,
Gloves clutching hot chocolate
With earmuffs to keep out the cold.
Snow angels and sculptures,
A blanket of white.
Thank You, my Father,
For the beauty of snow,
And for all the fun
We can have in it.

Amen.

Winter wonderland

The cold, crisp snow crunches underfoot,
The fire blazes bright,
Your breath hangs in the air,
Christmas decorations delight.

Mulled wine and mince pies
Always warm your toes,
Christmas music, specially carols,
Everywhere you go.

Christmas stories are retold,
Time and time again,
Sleeping children, tiny reindeers,
Rejoicing once again

At the birth of a baby,
Born inside a cattle stall,
Adored by Mary, shepherds, Wise men,
The One who saved us all.

These are the things I love
About winter, Christmas, the child,
Born to be our rescue
Who came from up above.

Snowscape

A glistening landscape,
White as cotton wool,
The snow packed tightly on the ground.
A lone snowman,
His face in a perpetual grin,
The half-eaten carrot that is his nose
Hanging lopsidedly,
Scarf, hat and gloves,
Placed on him.
The blinding glare of the sun,
Bouncing off the snow
And dazzling the eyes,
Changing the landscape
And calling for brighter days to come.
This is our white Christmas,
Of years gone by,
Celebrating and being thankful
For all we have,
Throughout the ages and into eternity.

Amen.

The donkey's journey

A donkey,
Walking steadily
Along a gravel track.
A lady, heavily pregnant,
Sitting upon his back.
Joseph, her husband,
Walking alongside,
Holding Mary while she
Sits,
Praying that her baby
Won't be born here,
But in Bethlehem,
Safe and sound.

Amen.

The Light

Light,
Piercing the darkness,
Blotting out the shadows,
Calling
Hope,
Dreams,
Visions
To life.
A love that surpasses everything,
Born in human form,
That we might know Him
As He knows us
And came so we might live again.

Amen.

Angels of hope

A star in the sky,
Angels singing,
The promise of life,
New hope from the ashes,
'A saviour has been born to you,
He is Christ the Lord.'
A blessing,
One to break the curse,
To defeat it,
'Why do you look among the dead?
He is alive!'
A chance to be made new,
Living life to the full,
Loved and accepted.

Amen.

The shepherds

The night He came,
We were astounded.
The lights,
The music,
The host of angels,
All singing Glory
And peace
And praising their God,
Our God,
So what else could we do?
The fire in our hearts drove us
To where He lay,
The Baby of Mary,
Our Saviour and Redeemer.

Amen.

Lucia

Light in the darkness,
Feet treading carefully,
Hands filled with wonders
Of food and drink.
A crown on her head,
The light spilling outwards,
Giving hope and life
To all she meets.
A living example
Of Daddy's love,
A daughter,
A martyr,
A friend to those in need.
May we remember,
On this Lucia,
To encourage others,
That they may succeed.

Amen.

Christmas trees

Spruce, blue as the sky,
Fir and pine, the green of the forest,
Adorned with lights
That sparkle and shimmer
In the darkness.
Angels and stars,
Wooden musicians playing,
Sometimes even...
Edible treats.
Baubles hung upon sturdy branches,
Tinsel, making us laugh as we place it,
Remembering Christmases before,
When we used to sing carols
And enjoy our Christmastime.

Amen.

Christmas markets

The crowds,
The lights,
The choirs singing carols.
Wonderful stalls
Filled with so many things.
Wolfing down mince pies,
A warm drink in your hand,
Soaking up the atmosphere
With family and friends.
Trying the food stalls
And listening to the singing,
Feeling blessed to be part
Of this every year.

Amen.

Christmas poem

Streets are bustling,
Choirs are singing,
The season of goodwill is here.
Christmas markets,
Filled with people,
Celebrating the time of year.
Snowy pictures,
Filled with beauty,
Decorating Christmas cards,
A season of love and peace
For everyone on earth at last.
Christmas turkeys,
Stuffed and ready,
In the oven on Christmas morn,
All to remember our King, Jesus,
The saviour of the world was born.
A little baby,
Born in a manger,
Shining for all the world to see,
Born to die,
That we might live,
Freedom abounding for you and me.

A grace,
A peace,
A joy is given,
Life beyond comparison,
A loving Father,
Watching His children,
The saviour of the world was born.
All glory be to Him in heaven,
And, upon this holy night,
May He look down with loving eyes
And keep you safe.
With that, goodnight!

The star

A star of beauty,
Streaking across the sky,
Announcing news
Of joy
And peace,
Life for us
All
And hope, living inside of us.
People stop and stare,
Gazing in awe and wonder
At the promise of redemption.

Amen.

Men of wisdom

A long journey,
The star guiding the way.
We travelled,
Guided by the promise
Of a King,
A King above all Kings,
One to whom
The world would bow.
A King of glory,
Compassion,
Love.
We thought ourselves wise,
Yet, when we saw Him,
We knew ourselves foolish,
For He held the wisdom
Of the One who saves our souls.

Amen.

Egypt

We came to the border
At dead of night.
Refugees from a tyrant,
Due to his jealousy,
And an escape to a land
That once persecuted us.
But then... a moment of peace,
An oasis for us,
As we held the hand
Of the child
That was born to save the world.

Amen.

The innocents

A scream,
A cry,
The thud of an axe.
Such senseless brutal violence,
All due to one boy,
A king's jealousy
And the order to kill.
Never let this happen
In our world again,
Father of all.

Amen.

Celebration

The business,
The bustle,
The last-minute rush,
Clamouring for presents,
Putting up decorations,
Making sure we're ready
For the big day,
His birthday,
Waiting with eager anticipation,
Getting closer by the second,
Till it's finally here,
Ready to be unwrapped
Till next year,
When it begins again,
Year after year,
As long as time goes on.

Amen.

The cornerstone

A gift,
Given for all,
Yet… rejected,
Cast aside, left
Outside
In the cold,
Snuggled in a manger,
Safe,
Protected,
Yet knowing where He was to go,
The ultimate sacrifice,
To be received by those
Who love Him.

Amen.

Love at Christmas

A time for indulgence,
Mince pies,
Christmas cake,
Friends and family gathering together.
Blazing fires,
Trees decorated with lights,
Tinsel strewn everywhere.
A time for dancing,
Carol singers at the door,
Bright colours
And love,
Born in a manger,
Crying and helpless,
Come to earth to rescue us
And set us free
Again.

Amen.

The visitor

He comes at night,
When all is dark,
With children fast asleep.
He whistles down the chimney
And then proceeds to creep
Into their bedrooms,
Attics,
Living rooms too,
To fill the stockings
One by one
And when, at last,
The job is done,
A mince pie or a piece of cake,
A carrot left, so he can take
It up to Rudolph,
Waiting there,
And once he takes off through the air,
He'll shout,
With such enormous glee,
'Merry Christmas to all,
But especially me!'

Amen.

Christmas day

The parcels opened,
The festive treats
All eaten,
The crackers pulled,
And the wine drunk.
That post-turkey stupor
Settles in,
Sitting in front of the TV,
Morecambe and Wise,
Queen's Speech,
Games are played,
A birthday remembered,
And all for a King,
Born in a manger,
Come to rescue us.
May we never forget
The reason
That we celebrate this day.

Amen.